Rainer Maria Rilke

The Voices

translated by
Robert Bly

Copyright Robert Bly 1977

Co-published in England by the Sceptre Press

Distributed by Bookpeople and Rainbow Bridge.

830
R4576E

Thanks to *The Minnesota Review*,
where these versions first appeared.

ISBN 0-915408-15-5 paper.
ISBN 0-915408-16-3 signed, handcased.

THE ALLY PRESS
Denver, Colorado

JUN 15 1978

THE VOICES
nine poems with a title poem

TITLE POEM

It's OK for the rich and the lucky to keep still,
no one wants to know about them anyway.
But those in need have to step forward,
have to say: I am blind,
or: I'm about to go blind,
or: nothing is going well with me,
or: I have a child who is sick,
or: right there I'm sort of glued together…

And probably that doesn't do anything either.

They have to sing, if they didn't sing, everyone
would walk past, as if they were fences or trees.

That's where you can hear good singing.

People really are strange: they prefer
to hear castratos in boychoirs.

But God himself comes and stays a long time
when the world of half-people start to bore him.

THE SONG THE BEGGAR SINGS

I go all the time from door to door,
scorched, soaked to the skin.
Then all at once I lay my right ear down
in my right hand.
Then my voice seems strange to me,
and I've never heard it like that!

Then I don't know exactly who is calling,
me or someone else.
I cry out about a cent or two,
the poets cry about more.

At the end using both my eyes
I close my face,
and when it lies with its weight in my hand
it looks almost like rest.
That's so they won't think I have nowhere
to lay my head.

THE SONG THE DRUNKARD SINGS

It wasn't really inside me. It came in and went again.
I wanted to hold it. But the wine was holding it.
(I've forgotten now, exactly what it was.)
Then he held this out to me, and that out to me,
till I was completely dependent on him.
I'm an ass.

Now I'm playing his game, and he throws me here and there,
wherever he pleases, and maybe today he'll lose
me to that pig, death.
When death has won the smudged-up card,
he will scratch his old scabs with me
and toss me in the heap.

THE SONG THE BLIND MAN SINGS

I am blind, you out there, that is a malediction,
an awful thing, a contradiction,
something heavy every day.
I lay my hand on the arm of the woman,
my gray hand on the gray of her gray,
and she leads me through empty spaces.

You move and push and like to imagine
that your sound is not like the sound of stone on stone;
however, you are wrong: I am the only one
who lives and suffers and has a sound.
I have endless scream in me,
and I don't know which is screaming, my heart
or my intestines.

Do you recognize my songs? You didn't sing them,
not quite with the stressing I use.
Every morning new light comes
warmly into the open house,
and you have a feeling that moves from one face to another,
and that leads you astray to caring.

THE SONG THE SUICIDE SINGS

Just another moment left!
But what they're doing to me, they're always taking the rope
and cutting it!
The other day it was so good!
And there was already a little bit of eternity
in my intestines.

They hold this spoon out to me,
this spoon of life.
Well I want it, and I don't.
I'd better throw up.

I know that life is just fantastic fun,
and the world is a foamy mug;
but I don't really get strength from it,
it just makes me dizzy.

It heals others, it makes me sick.
Grasp, that some can't stand it.
For at least a thousand years now
I'll have to fast.

THE SONG THE WIDOW SINGS

At first life was good to me.
It kept me warm, it gave me courage.
Of course it does that to all the young,
but how could I have known that.
I had no idea what life was—
suddenly it was nothing but year after year,
not good any more, not fresh any more, not wonderful any more,
as if torn in two pieces down the center.

It wasn't his fault, and it wasn't mine;
neither of us had much except patience,
and death didn't have any.
I saw him come (what an ugly sight),
and I watched him, while he took and took:
of course what he took wasn't mine.

What did belong to me then, what did I have that was mine?
Wasn't even my grief
only a loan from Fate?
Fate wants not only the happiness,
he wants the pain and the screaming back,
and he buys it all second-hand.

Fate was there and got for almost nothing
every expression on my face,
everything except the way I walk.
Every day he had a clearance sale,
and when I was empty, he walked out
and left the door open.

THE SONG THE IDIOT SINGS

They don't bother about me. They let me be.
They say, "Nothing can happen."
That's good.
Nothing *can* happen. It all comes and wheels
steadily around the Holy Ghost,
always around that same Ghost (you know) —

No, of course not, one mustn't think any *danger*
could come in that way.
Of course the blood exists.
Blood is the heaviest. Blood is heavy.
Sometimes I think I've had too much —
(That's good.)

O, isn't that a wonderful ball!
Round and red as it all.
Good thing that you created it.
But will it come, if you call?

How strangely the whole thing behaves,
into each other driving, out of each other swimming,
friendly, a touch uncertain.
That's good.

THE SONG THE ORPHAN SINGS

I am nobody, and I will be nobody too.
Now I'm too small to live, of course;
later it'll be the same.

Mothers and Fathers,
think of me.

Of course it isn't worth the trouble of raising me:
I will be mowed down anyway.
Nobody can use me: it's too early now,
tomorrow, too late!

I have only this one dress,
and it's getting thin and bleached,
however it will last an eternity
in the eyes of God.

I just have these few locks of hair
(they never change) that once
somebody loved.

Now he is through with love.

THE SONG THE DWARF SINGS

It's possible my soul is upright and OK;
but it can't make my heart stand straight
or my crooked blood — it's from those things
that the pain comes.
My soul has no place to walk in, no place to lie,
it catches on to my sharp skeleton
with a terrified beating of wings.

My hands will never amount to anything either.
See how stunted they are?
They're moist, they hop around sluggishly
like toads after a rain.
And everything else in me
is sad and old and worn-out;
why does God hesitate to throw it all out
on the dump?

Is he angry with me, perhaps, for my face
with its sullen mouth?
It was ready, so often, to be full
of light and clear deep through;
but nothing ever came as close to it
as the big dogs did.
And dogs don't have it.

THE SONG THE LEPER SINGS

I am one of those people whom everything has given up.
Nobody in the city knows that I exist.
Leprosy has happened to me.
And I strike my wooden clapper,
knock my sad themesong
into the ear of every person
who comes near.
And those who hear that sound, look
certainly not here, and what is happening here
they don't care to know.

As far as the sound of my clapper reaches, there
I am at home; but maybe
you're making my clapper so loud
that they won't trust my distance anymore
than they trust my nearness now.
I'm able to go a very long way
without coming on girl, woman,
child, or man.

But it bothers me when I frighten animals.

Born in Prague, 1875, Rainer Maria Rilke became one of the most influential poets in the early 20th century. The originality of his work transcends any one label, though he has been described as a mystic, neo-romantic, decadent and an expressionist. Until his early death in 1926, Rilke produced many volumes of correspondence and poetry, including his two most significant poetic statements about the human condition, *Duino Elegies* and *Sonnets to Orpheus*. *The Voices* is a section taken from *Buch der Bilder*, first published in 1906.

Robert Bly, an accomplished American poet, has published several volumes of translations including *Friends, You Drank Some Darkness — Three Swedish Poets*, *Neruda and Vallejo: Selected Poems* and *Lorca and Jimenez: Selected Poems*, all from Beacon Press. Among his recent small press publications are *Sonnets to Orpheus* by Rilke, Mudra Press, and *Try To Live To See This!*, versions of Kabir, by the Ally Press.

THE ALLY PRESS
$1.95